Charly Cox is a 22-year-old writer, producer and poet.

Her writing focuses on destigmatizing mental health and the coming-of-age of a young woman surviving the modern world. In January 2017, she published her first poem on Instagram, showing her internet followers her poetry for the first time; since then she's been asked to be Virgin Radio's poet in residence, she's been published on Refinery29, hosted poetry nights and been named by *ELLE* magazine as one of their 20 power players to watch out for in 2018. In March 2018, Charly was named as ambassador for MQ Mental Health, a charity which funds research into mental illness. *She Must Be Mad* is Charly's first book.

she must be mad

Charly Cox

*A mental coming-of-age documented through poetry and prose
written by someone who's still in the thick of it*

ONE PLACE. MANY STORIES

HQ
An imprint of HarperCollins*Publishers* Ltd
1 London Bridge Street
London SE1 9GF

This paperback edition 2018

3
First published in Great Britain by
HQ, an imprint of HarperCollins*Publishers* Ltd 2018

ISBN: 978-0-00-829166-2

MIX
Paper from
responsible sources
FSC˚ C007454

This book is produced from independently certified FSC™ paper
to ensure responsible forest management.

For more information visit: www.harpercollins.co.uk/green

Printed and bound in Great Britain by
CPI Group (UK) Ltd, Croydon, CR0 4YY

Contents

she must be in love / 3

she must be mad / 41

she must be fat / 77

she must be an adult / 113

For the men who broke my heart, for the beta-blockers that slowed it, and a chunk of what is left to the sisterhood with a gift tag wrapped around it reading: *let's try and figure this all out together.*

I owe this all to my madness and those who have suffered it. I never thought I'd be a poet. I never knew one day I'd slap a title on a cover that encased sometimes lonely and sometimes excited thoughts and say, 'Here it is! A book of poems! By me, Charly ... The Poet!' But life shocks you and here we all are. In that never tense, I didn't know a thing – I just knew how to feel. I took to feeling like a sport and I exercised every one of those achy heartstrings that had festered in cliché drivel until they snapped and aortic wells poured and shouted, 'For god's sake woman, can you just write these feelings down so we can have a break?' And so I did. For years in silence and secrecy. I wrote these poems and letters to my past self and in every sort of melodramatic, romantic, ridiculous way, these are what saved me. Saved me from an intensity I was afraid to share until I morphed them into something to share with you now. Some of these were written at sixteen, others at twenty-two; they were all written growing and lost and sad sunk, but they were also all written with eventual hope. A hope that I clung to in the most intense way that only a girl desperate to take a peek at womanhood, battling a wealthy portfolio of mental health issues nervously, could. Finding strength in the contention of such frustrated confusion, in odd and debilitating sadness, in jubilant first kisses and clangs of clarity – in the words of our lord saviour Britney Spears, 'I'm not a girl – not yet a woman'. And there is something truly quite almighty in that in-between … either that or, I must truly just be mad.

she must be in love

love part 1

Nobody ever tells you that there'll be comedians and poets, actors and academics, college students and forty-year-old men to fall in love with.

That you will fall in love with them all.

Their charm and their poise, their anecdotes and foreign phrases, even the stray scratchy hairs on their cheeks and chins that will tickle like an acrylic yarn against your youth.

They first come soft. Soft and slow and ethereal, these perfumed clouds of promise that smell new but hang old, and then before a single tendril has had time to make itself at home on your collar, they exit loud and angry and too early.

They will always exit too early.

Little-to-no explanation, a hole so deep you lose your feet to the black and bleak of self-assumed guilt, he flings the door on its hinges for another man to oil and mend.

You'll re-imagine hope until he leaves too, tarnishing his very own handiwork.

Nobody ever tells you of these good-looking silhouettes because they have stood in their cast before. They relished in the same way you will but they cowered in the flood.

They sunk with weakened limbs until they no longer knew of that initial burst and lay themselves down to surrender. You, however, will not allow yourself to be a casualty to love. You will grow stronger in it, if you try.

It's six minutes past midnight, Facebook has updated Messenger, video now available, you have no one to call.

Soon, it's twenty-one minutes past twelve and an unfamiliar noise rings through the hard plastic of your first laptop, it starts to screech. You look up and to the side, a rerun of the news now only important to your periphery.

A boy. It's a boy.

A boy you've never met but whose life you know the lengths of. Holidays, parties, girlfriends, new friends, birthdays, likes, lunches – all arranged into bite-sized books you've read and torn pages from time and time again. The boy. The boy from the holidays and the parties, with the girlfriends and the new friends, he's calling you. You answer.

Spanking new anticipation twirling twines that tie knots in your chest, frayed ends tickling your stomach to stir hot queasy butterfly soup.

'Hello.' He says, monotone. Northern.

Eyes thinning to an embarrassed sleepy squint.

'Hey?' You say, a question. Southern.

Smile curving to bunch the bags from under your eyes to pillows.

'Just wondered what your voice sounded like.' He says, he smiles back.

'Same. Now we know.'

Lights dim in both screens, you dissolve into the silence of each other's nights, minds reaching out to touch the other, tousle hair, feel skin. Talk. Talk. Laugh. Smile.

Embarrassment has gone.

It's five thirty-six in the morning four years later. Lights still dim, faces still rounded in the glow of the laptop. Girlfriends once stalked are now ex-girlfriends discussed. Holidays, planned as fleeting dreams of train journeys across the country to finally meet. Likes, shared. Sometimes agreed.

'Do we know, or at least think, that if you lived down the road from me we'd be in love?' He wrote.

'Yes.' You reply.

A life starts to lead along a parallel secret line, a life that's yours and a line of fibre optics. Two years pass. You meet in a newsagent at a train station. He's smaller than you thought. You're fatter than he'd seen. Geography offers different greetings. Kiss, hug, release. You share pancakes but struggle to look at each other. You walk across Battersea Bridge, he lights a spliff, you sit facing away from each other and imagine you're still just on the phone. Better.

Three years later and it has never happened again. You never found out if he became the poster boy for postmen in Salford. You never got to tell him of the new bosses and the trips to America. You never got to tell him all the things he was right about. You never got to tell him how your heart held out, how it still occasionally chooses to hold out. How in a life lived on a parallel secret line you never unplugged the receiver. But now you do. Now you get to tell him somewhere he might find it and can only hope he does, before he finds someone else.

to you

This feels silly to write
For in doing so
The sentiment fractures
And goes back full circle
But I've kissed plenty of boys
Most of them charming
I've kissed plenty of boys
And I've been on plenty of arms and
I've loved plenty of boys
And they've made me feel soft
And I've seen plenty of boys
And plenty I've lost
I've had plenty of evenings
In dimly lit bars
And I've had plenty of fumbles
In the backs of their cars
I've written plenty of letters
And received plenty of emails
I've kissed plenty of boys
And one or two females
I've traced plenty of hips
With eager touch
And I've kissed plenty of lips
That made me feel too much
And in the plenty I've gathered

I've garnered plenty of words
But once put all together
They don't sound like firsts
They all sort of sound similar
As though each man wasn't new
Which is why it's important to say
Not everything I write is about you.

she moves in her own way

It was sticky in your apartment
I stuck my eyes to every corner
Where you'd stuck up old postcards
An entire museum of your life and more a
Window
Framed the shrilling stuck-up summer silhouettes in the pub
    down below
You stuck a scratched record on
That played the once smooth staccato
You poured me a glass of wine
That slipped sticky to my sides
That slipped your fingers across my thighs
I felt stuck
This time I promised myself I wasn't giving up
You said stick around
And I cleared off the dark sediment red wine muck
From my lips
And kissed you in a way
That begged to reverse ownership
But instead it sellotaped my wrists
Together tight around your hips
Whilst my internal monologue screamed:

You're hopeless at this
You don't want to do this

You always do this
You don't have to be this
Person
You don't have to quench your thirst on
Him
Tell your body its anxiety isn't a passion to burst on
Him
Don't try and fill the void with empty consumption
This moment in time that you'll lie and say was sweet seduction
Was another episode of you orchestrating a personality reduction
Into a girl you have no business being
No pleasing being
Stop teasing feeling
From an inner drought
That only dried to be that way
Because you gave all your kindness out
Instead of spending it on yourself.

I stop as your eyes unstuck from mine
You swig from the bottle of wine
And I muster up the courage to say
I don't want to be *just* tonight
I've said it before and let it be denied
And you laugh with a cocksure sigh
And hit me with another line like
Why can't you just be a girl for a good time?
And it's the just that juts

And ricochets

And it slaps stuck

To my ongoing conflict with myself

                         I reach for a souvenir placed on your shelf

Throw it between my palms

Imagine what false comfort I'd find within your arms

And put it back

I give learning from lessons a crack

I stop myself from telling you that you're such a twat

When you text me the next morning

To say my excuse as a woman is appalling

For leaving in a rush

It was sticky in your apartment

And it was there that I realised

I was bored of being stuck

As a girl whose muchness amounted to just

The night.

mourning routine

He is unsmoked cigarettes
And lukewarm tea
A morning routine
(He's) not consumed by me
A craving that will fade
Left unfinished in the sink
Until my wine-stained lips
Call the next round of drinks

I'll wake up in the morning
Next to someone new
But I still fell asleep
Hoping that someone would be you.

mesh of kisses

Find the contented without the contention of giving away half of
    yourself
And see that letting go isn't giving in
But a spiritual commodity of wealth
My best teachers were disguised as lovers
Unmasked when I untangled their mesh of kisses
And smothered myself instead with the notion that they were
    knowledgeable near misses
And Mr Brave
The future without the listless lustful nights
Replaced with a silhouette of love
That was bred from moulding a mistreated wrong into its
    rightful right.

anatomical astrologist

Your body became so familiar
I touched your skin the same way I'd fumble down the side of
    the TV in the dark and know the difference between the
    <off switch> and the <volume button>
Each line and freckle a constellation on your torso
        I could read backwards like an anatomical astrologist.
           We intertwine and I sigh softly
          a shared unspoken bedtime language that
             screamed
             to the gods for just
              five
              more
             minutes
    Time stopped to matter and the matter of us across your old
      mattress pulled apart until your stars dimmed down to
      flickering filaments and I chose to switch them off.

otters

It is what it is until it isn't
Quite it anymore
Makes perfect logical sense, sure
But in eleven short words I don't think you swirl the score
Of what I'm on about
I could mutter an uttering of offers
Words that cling to syllables as tightly as otters
In love
Did you know they never let go once they've found a mate?
Did you know that my slithering of truth wasn't yours to emanate
Dissipate, dissolve upon your lips
As my truth became a movement and your hands became my hips
In a haze of a few Sundays
Of what I thought was it
But didn't know that it could be something just one of us could quit
And that's quite exactly it
It was what it wasn't
Instead of a smattering of emails that will one day be forgotten
Instead of a flattering string of inhales that sung kindly until
    coughed out rotten.
Again these are all just words
Silly sold sentiments aren't that tough
I could rhyme anything together and it'd still be enough
For you to know what I'm wittering on about is love

It is what it is until it isn't
Quite it anymore
It's tracing your finger on a back
That will soon traipse out the door
It's wine on a Saturday and lies that you learn as foreplay
It's lust in its golden hour
It's kissing goosebumped in the shower
It's handing over innocence to a dastardly power
Of frightening fragile fragments that someone can stack in their
     own tower
No choice in whether it cements a building for their ego or a
     fence around a field of flourishing flowers
All grown for you
It is what it is until it isn't quite it anymore
Until you become loathsome for the quibbling quirks of comfort
And love writes as a rule to deplore
Makes perfect logical sense, sure
Until the it that isn't and the was that wasn't
Is just a silhouette of your insecurity
And truly nothing more.

weight of you

As my body writhes around a different bed
It feels taller even though it's not
Semi-clothed and cold it feels different
But not lonely
It feels older and as though it knows further and fresh
It learns less of you and no wider of me
But it understands something new
That isn't uncomfortable
It just wants to find you again and for you to know me once more
And for that once more to see what I wished you'd seen before

Before it would cry out a screech of heart strung bedlam
Lying with a bread-bloated belly that looked pregnant
Pregnant with the thought of you
Coming back to bed soon
But you didn't

Different cities and marbled skies
Slow the pace between us
And Indian spices heat the burn our tongues loved together
But now saffron and chai
Taste an unsavoury uncleanness

There is no loneliness to chew
Just a space in the creases of linen
That should belong to the weight of you.

lipstick

Let me kiss you close mouthed
Let me rouge your bitter cheeks
With this darker red
Let me wrap the gentle curve of my body
Into someone else's bed
I'll let you wipe the cherry plum stain off
With the memory of when you said
'Cheer up sweetheart, the thing with
People like you, is they'll only love you
When you're dead.'

lovebites

I hadn't noticed it at first
It was done with such kindness
It hadn't thought to hurt
But as I stumble off the train
With my knickers hitching my skirt
It would've been nice to know of the night
That instead of just leaving my phone charger behind
I'd be taking away a lovebite
A 'hickey'
A purple blue yellow not nearly skin-coloured enough to cover
With make-up
Tricky
Situation
Learning to flatten my tones from their guilty high fluctuations
When I say
It's eczema?!

At school a girl had one on her head
And said
She'd headbutted a cupboard
And cut in a fringe before the teachers had discovered it
Is *so* silly that they must be hidden
That something which once brought pleasure
Is suddenly forbidden
Like, *grossly* forbidden

Like, I walked into a party and everyone was shocked
That I was either bursting with pride
Or should be embarrassed that I'd forgot
To slap on some concealer
Or that I was akin to a slapper who'd hooked up with a drug dealer
Which for the record would be fine
It's my neck to be decorated by whomever I desire
Minutes of passion holstered to a circle
That gets flashed every now and again
Like being autographed with a biological purple pen
It's a bruise from a kiss
Not a place keeper for a fist
Just a splodge of romance stamped profoundly pissed
It's as fleeting as the youth we're scared to miss
As it's administered
I struggle to cast it off as something sinister

And for whatever attention they seem to seek
I'm happy to laugh in their existence
And thank *god* that they only last a week.

with his assistants

She squirms nearly naked beside me
Lollipop stick legs
Like a Lowry
Waiting to be coloured
I fill her in best I can
With a haze-hugged recital
Madness over just one man
It splutters slurred and sloppy
I feel her skin soft and on me
She breathes a sigh drenched in
Yawns for coffee
We put on one of his shirts together
Find the slunked-off socks
And bury down secrets we now have to keep forever
His face is unimaginable
He'd have guessed it sooner
Had his lust been made more tangible
But he was busy
When we were busy for him.

doubletree by hilton

Mesmeric in the most disarming demanding way
I flash honesty brazen and wasted
As you kiss the words from out my mouth as though they're still
    untasted
Satiated
We lay
As you press your head upon me and lie about my beauty as
    though it's your unspoken duty
I feel safe because you've said it
Feel a rush of adrenaline and then push it from my head
You said it
I watched you close your eyes and forget it for a second
And then deny it
You falsify your worth with memories unjust
You try nothing more than to make me feel I was once untouched
And now all I want
Is for the history before us
To erase in diluted drops
That you slipped along my index fingers
When in this heat my rings got stuck.

porn

She moans
As he throws
Her body
From arched feline back
To face in the pillow on her tummy
He pulls her by the ponytail
Her eyes widen with excitement
Loneliness
As well
Banshee screams and hollow slaps
Perfect nudity and waxed arse cracks
Half taken by the throng of flung-off thongs
I'm bemused and sad and thinking
Why do they never show the naps?
The intimate legs twined like spaghetti
Cooked and thrown back in the pack
Stuck with starchy love
That's the real magic, that
That's what turns me on
When after all the sheets have seen
Where you lay and nose touches nose
And you still know where to kiss
With the lights still off
Because you're lit up in a childlike beam
And through panting pause your mind wanders lost

Feeling your skin cling innate to one another
Like a baby to a breast
                      That first breath
When you exhale and simmer,
Two maudlin corpses
Too hot and they still shiver
Craving more whilst digesting a slither
Of moments ago

She moans
As he throws
Her body
Wanting it with a posture comfy
He runs his fingers through her hair
And tells her that she's lovely
Beautiful in fact
He grabs her by the waist
As she holds his face
And steadies gaze
Whispers lightly in his ear
I'd rather make love to you
Than just simply let you fuck me

There is plenty of room for explicits in complicity

Now *that* I'd understand
A prude I'd never claim to be

Though nor a connoisseur of wild intimacy
I've always taken it how it's given to me
… directed it occasionally
But there's something that seems strange to me
That we get off on a close-up of a staged aggressive filthy
When we all know in reality
The best is sweet and purely
Ends the same
The two of you, vulnerable and glowing
With the taste of each other's name.

evolution

Days later
Paint-like
Each layer peels
And falls from my lips
That you bit
And thus become features
That are no longer owned by your kiss.

snapple lid facts

An octopus has three hearts
How does he find time to use them?
Dexterous in his tentacle touch
It must be hard to know what's a tickle from abuse to them
What space there is for entertaining a mermaid or a sea urchin
He doesn't have to unpick beauty from sense or smarts from lust
He can just drink them all up
In a salty ablution
And sit drunk
Sounds nice but
I bet it's secret emotional hassle
I bet he'd prefer to slurp a sluice of Snapple
What decisions are necessary to make when there's a home for
    each mistake
All kept warm and left unsearching
How does he find time to use them when he needs it all just to
    keep them working?
Keep each beat in syncopation
Without disrupting the sea's heady and unforgiving intention
Selling him gravelly bits of information
As he presses his ear to a shell
How does he decide what's worth keeping or best shelved?
How does he pick what's right and fulfilling
When he's got three beating organs never fit to burst or to be
    pained and unspilling

How does he feel anything
When he's got capacity for so much?
Squirming neatly on the sea bed
He stretches out to disturb the dust
Half swim half sleep he imagines what it would be like to be us
How simple it could be
To reserve all of his energy
Into just one place to love.

kaleidoscope

As you bashed my eyes from blue
These distorted shapes were carved by you
Until swiftly all I saw judged hope
As you threw me in your kaleidoscope
Pushed down a misted barrel lens
Creasing wraps and crushing tenths
Squinting smiles as you kissed wrists
and squaring miles on homebound trips
I wandered calm for months before
Became the girl you swore unsworn
And now headfirst it smacks me clean
You conjured colours I can't see
A fool I often am
But tonight a fool I'll gladly be.

rosie cheeks

It smells as delicious
As my mind told me so
And as its thorns graze my thigh
I apologise before its beauty
And cry not for pain
But for getting too close
To something much more delicate than I
And not expecting to leave bloodied.

app cheats

Their names together wash over me
Syncopated
Hypnotic
Tepid water rushes through my sinuses
Until it heats to a gentle boil
Slow bubble, rising
To sit along my lash line
As a stagnant source
Awaiting provocation
Syncopated
Hypnotic
Vindicated and
Neurotic
I almost wanted them to
Sound like a flood
I scrounge for photos of
Them in love
I rip through feeds
And rehash texts
And play out what
He didn't say next
As though he did
I am crazed by the drama
That has been denied
And scroll through three years of holiday photos
That he profiled as a lie.

first west service

He pressed his palms against my breasts
On a crowded bus
Cradling the darkness in my head
Until it felt like it was just us
And when we got back to his
In solitude we could melt
I went to tell him who I was
But learnt he wasn't there for how I felt.

You sit with your tongue pained out of your mouth like an artist, bottle of stolen rum from your parents' cabinet in one hand and an emptied bottle of water between your thighs.

Don't. Spill. Anything.

You learned only last night that Malibu has a particularly unforgiving stench when left to soak in carpet. Neatly, you tuck it into your school bag, pocket four pound coins from your father's parking meter compartment in his Volvo estate and head to school on a cold Friday morning. The night is young. The night is so young you're checking for spillage in double maths and texting a boy from the school down the road 'wuu2 tonight?' with one eye on algebra and the other on your LG Shine phone. You know what he's up to.

It feels like the longest day of your life, in hindsight nothing really does ever feel as long as today. You are a worthy warrior that fights each pounding heart thump of anxious anticipation in her stride, you valiantly navigate the hours with nothing but a muted floral bodycon skirt and silk low-cut top awaiting to be loaded as ammunition. The day dribbles off into the later afternoon and you salivate to evening, thirsty dry mouth puckering in your mother's lipgloss. The prolonged MSN chat has been aching, tension-building, near nausea. Tonight you'll have your first kiss. You know it, you can see it, you have dreamt enough *Angus, Thongs and Perfect Snogging* scenes, it will be tonight. It must be. You feel so terrifyingly far behind that if it's not, womanhood will never greet you. You are not a girl nor a woman, you are an unwanted potato in a packet, left to half-freeze too close to the back of the fridge. It must be tonight. The process prior is almost ceremonial, the half a beer that leaves you giddy is a toast to the gods of fate, the borrowed pair of tanned tights is your celebration wear, the panic attack in the locked bathroom of the party before you've met is a nod and a vow to the severity of the process. It's all quite dumb, all quite ridiculous, all quite right. The party is quickening in pace, the toilet door you have bolted is being kicked at to make way for an early casualty of apple sours, you steady your defences and anchor a root in a confidence you have grown in that moment. Animalistic in your approach, you sidle past each faux drunken swaying body, pushing through a living room, a kitchen, and then to a garden with purpose. There he is. Too tall in his body he has not yet grown into, he leans on a trellis in the rain. You say your name at him like a greeting. He nods, accepting, watching your Bebo user flash before his squinted eyeline. You talk. It is all so unbearably awkward that you look for other familiar faces you can slope off with. You slope off with him. Backs against a forgotten Wendy house, you kiss. It's unlike anything. No metaphor, no simile, no book you read too young. It's tongues and hot flushed panic, it's anxiety boiled to a surface of pure sugar resin that you bite from each other's lips. It's a morishness sans lust, it feels innate. It feels as though there is an end point you must discover but you only have the tools to enquire and not conquer. It is feeling without thought for the first time. It's delicious – brief flashes of mortified and embarrassed – but delicious. No kiss will ever be the same. Some more prolific, some more dramatic, some more regretful, some more meaningful. But none the same. None more swift and intoxicating. None that was so unashamedly stenched with a mud-stained half hangover that when you head to text him the next morning, the ambush of 'WAHEEEEEEEY!!! I SAW YOU LAST NIGHT!!' splashed across your Facebook wall lights you with unabashed pride that nothing else will ever give you. You later realise, much much later, that the grin that lasted for weeks was the end of all those months of feeling like 'the fat friend', 'the nerd in disguise', 'the uncool one', 'the forgettable one'. They were all sad endured lies because within those was 'the girl that would never be kissed'. And she was. And she would be again.

the first time

Numbed nerves and conceited confidence
We fall into a depth of expectation
Familiarity grins back at us
And it laughs
And we laugh
Complexities lace around your features
Truth curling through my tongue
Slicing through a mist of excitement
Spilling to curdle into bittersweet reality

Mistaken as a mistake

As your slow body collapses
Next to me I watch your mind spin
Tentative teeth caging your thoughts
Until we digress into secrets
Misjudged, misinterpreted, mishaps

We are wondering
You are lost and I have lost.

love part 2

Love is going to smack you in such a way you don't recognise it, from the hands of a man whose fingers you wouldn't trust on a trigger. Love isn't what you thought. It's not what you were ever expecting. In your twenties, naked body sprawled across someone's bathroom, throwing up all within you, listening to the clink of plates as he toasts you crumpets having just cleaned up your mess, you muster, 'I love you.' Weird. Uncomfortable. What?! It's all too much to fathom. Surely you can't be that basic? It changes.

One night, when you are in his bed, his hot sticky breath scalds your skin with a thick jamminess, it prickles quick temperate flashes along your neckline and you begin to cry. You reimagine all the times he stopped to take your photograph. 'What are you doing? I look so gross, stop it. What sort of memory is this?!' You'd bat, pulling strands of hair from behind your ears over your face to hide. 'It's only for me!' Only for him? You could never quite grasp why anyone would want a collection of pictures of you with burnt rosacea red cheeks, often hungover, in his pyjama tops, in budget cafés, until right now. It stings you as he leans to kiss you and you can't pucker because all you can do is cry. It's not really even a cry, it's a sob. A snot on your chin, belly aching screech of water works. He is confused. His gentle comforting strokes force your body rigid. 'I'm fine, I'm fine, just change the song. It always makes me sad.' This is partly true. The other part loops behind your eyelids as you press them into the pillow as he panic searches for something new. It won't stop.

Never had an end been so grotesquely visceral. Never had a projected moment of foresight clung to your brain as though nothing else would ever be more true. When would anyone sit and look through such bizarre, such random, such inane photos?

When you were no longer there.

You see his limbs half in and half out, snaked around his duvet weeks from now. His finger pinching to zoom, swiping furiously through months. Looking at all these moments that at the time you thought were nothing of note but now are all that remain.

The tears slowly start to lessen, he gives you a lost stare and you offer a half smile. Dimples that suggest you know you're being silly. Silly for crying over 'a song'.

But in reality, there was not an ounce of silliness or stupidity to your reaction. You'd planned tomorrow's walk, you'd planned the lunch you'd attempt to eat, you'd planned the words you'd say to him, to explain this wasn't working any more, you had planned the whole damn thing and suddenly in a wisp of an unexpected thought, all those plans unravelled and you won't stomach it for weeks.

Even now, looking back, thinking on the countless photos taken after that night, you wished you'd taken some too. You wished you'd smiled in a few. You wished you'd had half the heart you had that night to have made an effort or, at least, to have been honest sooner.

Love is also continued frustration. It's anger. It's hurting. It's denying it for months and only seeing its presence, for the first time, in a memory. It is not always just the butterfly chase that you expected. Sometimes it's also resentment. It's embarrassment. It's putting all of your dreams on hold, totally swept in not realising. It's endurance. It's anguish. It's not what you wanted, not what you went looking for in your absent search for the next thing. It's intoxicating, it's routine, it's hard goddamn work. But they don't tell you that. Or maybe they do. Maybe you weren't listening. Maybe you were hanging off the end of a feeling late night WhatsApps gave you. Hanging off the end of movies, of prematurely-written poetry you'd penned in hope of one day arriving there with a person. It's horrid. It's gross. It's real and it stinks in a romantic putrid parma violet sweetness. So today you hate yourself for thinking you knew what love was but when it arrived you couldn't send it back quick enough. Laying in your pants on the sofa with last night's curry reheated screaming to no one but the ceiling.

'I DIDN'T ASK FOR THIS. THIS ISN'T IT. HOW DO I RESIGN?'

But no matter how many times you swipe with wool-gathered ease through Tinder praying to erase it, no matter how many times you tweet your soul is a dark expanse and your heart is a gothic black cave in as many self-depreciating retweet-worthy characters, it isn't. Your heart is filled with chest banging love and there is absolutely nothing you can do about it and that is it. Love is 'that is it' even when you feel like it isn't.

she must be mad

mind part 1

You remember, quite explicitly, the moments all of the weight first felt tangible. Your best girlfriend from school blimps in on MSN, 'I love you but I don't think I can help you anymore.' Each word sinks and anchors ground to the pit of your stomach and steadies your defences. She is right. A week later your best male friend bikes in the snow to your house at two-thirty in the morning and you let him cradle you as your apologies splutter out with a stench of lavender bleach. Weeks before, scissor scores sloped around the shapes of the tips of your fingers so you could no longer hold a pen on exam day. You lay, heavy in limbs and mind, cursing that no one else had ever felt this way. No one could understand. There wasn't a name for you, so you create a face instead. Bright and brash, loud and lovely – you walk into every room with conversation, jokes, anecdotes, bold red lipstick, and funny styled hair. You swig from bottles of wine and ring in every party as the go-to girl for a good time. It is much easier this way. Nobody has to know. MSN has long folded, your teeth cleansed from bathroom cleaner, the hard skin on your hands now, just simply, interesting. It's a charade that becomes so well-scripted, lovingly rehearsed, articulated in mirrors of bars before re-entering, that often it is hard to decipher which part of you is acting. You forget so quickly in those performances, of the excruciating pain, the sobbing, the fast heart racing to leap from out your chest via your mouth and spluttered in bile before you can leave the house. You deny yourself that those moments were true and that they ever happened. You attend doctors' appointments, pop pills, dutifully research a Wikipedia file of celebrities with 'bipolar II', scream at your friends, scream at the chemist, scream at the man in the bloody corner shop, scream at yourself that even though the weight still feels tangible, it can't be real. You are solemnly bored of pity, of being bedridden … of performing. Advisors come and go, all wearing different masks, some lovers, some friends, some professionals, your costume remains the same until one day you sit in front of a girl with deep purple hair and pink lipstick. She orders you a bowl of mash potato and a side of broccoli, an espresso and a Bloody Mary. She holds your hand and tells you the one thing that everybody else had given you with guilt but this time gives it to you as a gift. It feels warm, it's cosy cuddled relief. It's the truth and this time it isn't lonely.

'You're not well. You're ill. You're suffering. It's all real, all of this. I'm here to help you see it through.'

'she must be mad'

They called me many things
In many places
All well-intentioned
Muffled nouns spluttered from kind faces
Adjectives
Then descriptors
Ushering packets of pills and tales of other strong victors
Sympathetic sighs and brushed smiles
With trying advice to dissolve difficult enmeshed vices
They all said things would get better
To treat this thing as a workable quirk and not an evil personal
    personality vendetta
That I had in for myself
Try loving yourself
And when you do tell others how
The journey you've been on is another girl's now
Another kid just like you pressing their brain shouting owwww
The honesty will hurt a bit, it might make you sad
But ignite a spark that burns brighter
Than all of the times you heard
'She must be mad',
Ignite a spark that burns brighter
Than all of the hurt
To smile
'Yeah, I guess I am, but it isn't all bad.'

Ignite a spark that burns brightest
From all of the dirt
The dribbling tear-sodden thirst
To drink to the girl you knew
She must be mad but my god she's brave too.

@saintrecords

When sanity seems so far

And guarded by gates made of worries

I thank a god

I wish were true

For Solange's Instagram stories.

doctor, doctor, don't help me
(written aged 15)

I think I crave rejection
And self-sabotage days
I like the way they taste
In their smokey beer cross haze
I like to feel this empty
To make some time for pain
Nothing drives me more crazy
Than the breaks of feeling sane.

selective feeling

Sometimes I forget I'm totally insane
But then I'll start to hear voices
And remember again
I don't want to be crazy
But sometimes there's comfort
In that's my word for lazy
Or sad
Or defeated
Or bouncing off walls
And I think if I wasn't
I'd find myself bored.

I wish I'd not spent so long crying in bed

I fear too much
To quantify the rest
To feel the beat
With flat palms on my chest
I fear too much
To think back to
When I wanted less
I fear too much
To see the mess
Of how much time I wasted
When I had plenty left.

rapid cycling

You put stars in my shoes
And clouds in my head
I'd chase the moon
If I could get out of bed

If I could slap my feet flat
On the floor
And walk towards
What you allotted yesterday
You hand me my fleeting allowance
Of disgruntled energy
So I can feel the thick winter air
Like a cold second skin
That blows through the splinters in the trees
And the cracks you've chiseled within

The fluctuating curves of bowing branches
Are the sunken eyes nestled under furrowed arches

You gift a still minute
And then gallop off with it
Always a step ahead
And just a scant visit.

funny

I feel *funny*.
Not like when – the light bounces from the sky
And you feel heat stroke from the sunny
Days of closing in on jokes
That girl is intelligently witty she's so *funny*
I feel done in
Funny 'ha ha's speak no fun
In the language I have learnt
Funny feelings aren't the taste of a jovial summer's eve descending burn
A *funny* feeling is a feeling of a leaf I'm scared to turn
A *funny* feeling is me seething at a friend
Who didn't mean to hurt
Me, I'm a bit funny that way
Funny isn't laughing at a joke I heard you say
Funny is me cramping in the lungs and wincing
I'm okay
Funny is the last thought before I sleep
Funny is the impression of me that you'll keep
Funny is the unexplained, self-contained
Anxiety of breathing
Grabbing my coat before closing
Because I feel *funny* as I'm leaving
That's why I'm leaving
I feel strange

A finger couldn't pinpoint it and words cannot explain
The curse of feeling *funny*
And knowing you've got yourself to blame
And still being unaware.
I took my pills this morning, I promise you I swear
The capsules grin at you in blister packs
And eyeless they still stare
They laugh at you
Like you've said something *funny*
There's no lies that you can throw at them
There's no amount of money

No words you can scream
                              Out
                                    Bluntly.
I've tried

Feeling so *funny* that funny isn't hysterical
So why am I crying hysterical tears?
Funny was something I'd always liked
So why does this *funny* feeling punch me with spite?
A funny feeling used to be the swig of a third pint
So why does feeling *funny* swing the last throw in my own fight?
If I stopped feeling *funny* maybe I'd get some sleep at night
I wish someone had shown me left when *funny* started to feel right

And I suppose the funny thing is that in life
First we laugh
And then we cope

First we mould aching into satire
And then claw our way into a hope
That the lumps in our throats, the inhalers tucked in pockets of coats
The fraying yarns on the tether of our metaphorical ropes
Don't really exist
But they do, I know they do.
And I think they deserve a more raucous applause
Than the monotonous bang of therapists' doors
Or the bedlam screams on bedroom floors
Or the wincing pinches of scissor scores
Funny no longer feels right
Because there is no comedy show in sight
This is real life
And the word is depression
The medical phrases should be shouted in succession
Because for all the days they've made my face nameless
It would help in abundance for them to be shamed less
For me to call them out for who they are
And I know it's wonderful that we've come this far
Forgive me
But
It's unhealthy for us to stick with
Dancing around a denial that nicks its
Legitimacy from camouflaging its pain
Even though I'm the one who picked it
Saying 'I feel Funny' just isn't the same
But I didn't pick this

I was my own brain before this
And that, as a human, I deserve to reclaim
In whatever funny sort of way I can.

I prescribe you this

The best sort of revenge is to be kind to yourself
To burden yourself with living another day
With nourishing yourself when it feels like you're not worthy
Sabotage the saboteur
Poison the punisher
With positivity
I try and anger unhappy me
With good thoughts
With slow breathing
I cut my teeth on seething
Searing hot flash panics
It's become so familiar
I feel uncomfortable when things aren't bad
It's
Complex
I want the darkness to know it's wanted
But I want my soul to feel less haunted
So I open up
And double bluff
Until synapses sizzle
And confuse self-harm
With self-love.

I know that truth is always beautiful
But this is something else
These are the chronicles
Written out from hell

These are the minutes we keep secret
The times we wished we were someone else
I know that truth is always beautiful
But this is something else
These are the smudged wings of angels
That we'd erase with second chances
These are the fleeting second glances
That led to the stale and baneful
Excuses for not feeling the same
I know that truth is always beautiful
But this is something else
This is a slice of honest living
I wish I could have dressed up for myself.

all I wanted was some toast

I got a fork stuck in the dishwasher
And now I can't stop crying
Whoever said depression was glamorous
Had clearly never considered dying
Over a peanut butter covered utensil
And that's not the worst of all
The wet clothes hanger fell over
So I punched my fist into a wall
I'd rather smell than have a shower
The thought of socialising is scary
I can't even binge on chocolate
Because 'happy me' cut out dairy
This is boring, I feel knackered,
All I wanted was some toast
But if I can't even handle that
I'm obviously going to die alone.

a voice I know

My thoughts run through unpredictable themes
Sometimes it's two conscious streams at once
Sounds fun, huh?
Sounds a bit like drugs, no?
Sounds like in a predominantly losing game of tapping in on our
    own brains
I've accidentally genetically placed my bets and won
Sometimes I don't shun
It
Sometimes there's some fun in it
Sometimes it's nice to look in from the outside
And still stay warm
But other times it's like being one in a team of screaming aggressors
And trying to bat away the swarm
That I've assembled
Sometimes it's like punching confidently bare-knuckled
And still being the one that falls down and trembles
Sometimes I don't know who I am
Most of the time I don't know where I stand
And it's in that exact spotlight
It all comes rushing in:
'You don't deserve him!'
'… Wait no, you're cooler!'
'What is this fatty casing around your limbs?'
'… Stop prodding it, you're much smaller

Than you believe!'
'You've got no point in this world!'
'… Shut up, that's your confidence thief!'
'You should stay in bed!'
'… You should take on the world!'
'You look silly in this dress!'
'… When did I become this beautiful girl?'
'You don't know your facts!'
'… Oh my god, you're on fire!'
'He was looking at her not you.'
'… What's not there to be desired?'
It's all a constant conflict
That speeds in every thought
When I don't feel so great
It draws a pencil line above my head
Much shorter than before
It's a voice that refuses to see growth
And then backtracks for a minute
And shouts that I'm taller than most
Sometimes I need it to hear my own stupidity
And sometimes it knocks a sizeable crack in my mental fragility
Sometimes it feels like an illness
And other times it feels like a super ability
When I'm alone it's easy to forget I am
Because someone else is nattering away
And if I had control of at least one of these voices
I've got no idea what I'd say

But maybe, it would be
Right or wrong
Fat or thin
An inbetween of all these things
They'll quieten down when you realise
You're as strong to be so tough
To see that all of you's
Enough.

wonder of worry

We become the wonder of worry
Greasy in apologies
Slithering around each other's truths
In a perfect eight-shaped double-headed noose
Beer-foamed lips catch glints
And glisten sticky awaiting calm
That wills to be administered mouth to mouth
As hands cover eyes and fingers rest in their brows

We become the wonder of worry
Wandering straight-edged
Slack-lined, tongues untied, holding
On to strawberry-coloured embarrassed
Pink in the cheeks that we rouged from the tint of our hearts, hapless
In spirit and gesture
Cursing our history for being a chemical-stained mess
But as you hold me in the crook of your arm and kiss my bruised head
Our madness weighs a little less

The wonder of worry is
Teeth teetering trips of silence
Locked lockets swinging open unasked
Wittering over an expectation of now and love passed
Past a parameter to shut down
Slow down, bend down and under through branches we've extended
Piling them high and climbing to a peak of united front splendid

We become the wonder of worry
A little lost in the unexpected
But as we wonder together the worry becomes fragmented
Halved and shared and further afloat
There is a crescent smile on our lips
And there's nothing left to clear in our throats.

amber meal

Wipe a slick of whiskey from your lips

The burning bitter now a tender kiss

It is a supper of divine, an amber meal

A glass to clink that dins out how to feel

And when we fall back together again

Which I'm certain shall be friends

against the odds

Please know

This crash

        And cool of rocks is now my home

Because you left me here to climb alone.

I thought it wicked

To offer out a space within you without offering its limit

To dilute down all the hours by leaving in a minute

I thought you wicked

But in a mess of this elixir

I still want you to see my splendour and lie within it.

unidentified businessman

Did you see his eyes?
The way he looked at me
I've seen that look before
In doctor's receptions and caught them in glass door reflections
That inward moment you look outward to seek a connection
With yourself through someone else

Did you really see them?
Blink and you'll miss it
A piece of ocean blue and an iris sunk in spirit
Querying a view of judgment so explicit
That you want to hold their two pearly glass pebbles
And extract all of their battled past trembles
And kiss it
Smooch the notion of their preconceptions
Cradle an ounce of the perfect they see as imperfections
And make them look the other way
Shoot back a glance
That knocks their sallow tin man stance
To ricochet
To hand on your heart hand over your heart just for a minute in his day
A head nod that doubles as a 'I hope you'll be okay'.

Did you see his eyes?
The way he looked at me

I've seen that look before
And selfishly I've greeted them by staring at the floor
Cracking a stranger's reality into one that's ignored
Walking on embarrassed and showing no remorse
All he wanted for a second was a moment out of the self-
    deprecated and absorbed
Moments we all live in

I saw his eyes and the way he looked at me
This time with no pause for thought or time to breathe
I looked down deep into those cerulean pools
Sighing a sympathetic offering of stealth
I saw the look in his eyes and there looking back was myself.

mind part 2

Sat upright in a bed that's not your own, you syphon through packets of medication. You study each pill, piercing the foil carefully, listening to each pop, placing them delicately in your palm. They build and build until you cannot hold any more without them slipping from between your fingers and so you start to put them in your mouth. Powdery and metallic in taste, you let them fur on your tongue. You clench down your teeth.

Swallow.

There is no method here, no meditation, no ideal or thought-out end. You just do. You swallow and swallow and swallow until you feel your eyes pulse distorted black shapes onto the wall in front of you. What are you doing? You're not sure. In its greatest irony this is the closest to alive you've felt in months. The power. The power that you'd thought these very things had taken from you now reclaimed in a moment of adrenaline-filled weakness. Your fingers and toes shake furiously, your heartbeat in your ears, your stomach dropping from higher storeys with each breath. You try so desperately to close your eyes, pushing your back slowly down the middle of the bed but they're forced open. Stapled. Prized and widening with fear. What have you done? How did you get here? Why?

No answer sizzles to the surface, just aggressive acid reflux. Vomit. Most of it down your top and stuck in your hair. Nonplussed you are still here. Then, tears. Duvet-gagged screams. Anxious pleading text messages to recipients of such absurdity as you've forgotten who you have. If anyone might care. You stay awake for days. Leaving early in the morning you close the front door halfway as to not wake anyone and you slip off to a shopping centre. Zombie-like fingering through clothes that just hours ago you tempted to never wear again, you buy them all. Dresses, make-up, books. Laden with distraction. Eyes still pulsing. Body tested to its final limits. Still working. Still pushing. Still alive. You arrive home silent. Curtains drawn, own bed. Two slices of dry toast. Vomit, again. You wriggle down and shut your eyes. Inner monologue shouting verses of your stupidity, angry and abusive phrases others have given you stuck to your mind's tongue, spitting it back as though it's language you have bred. It's not. Your phone vibrates. Anxiety. You haven't dared to read the things that you had sent. The panic of others' worry. The fear of who you may have hurt in hurting yourself. The gross indulgence of asking for help from someone so removed. Expecting someone to care. Your body writhes around in filth and shame. It is not until now that you realise what you've done. The weight of it all. The seriousness. This act of punishment administered so nonchalantly that it evokes terror each time you remember it. Why did it feel so innate? Why was it so easy? If no obvious trigger, who's to say the same again is not a sleepwalk away.

You open the message, it reads:

The reality you experience in your head is secondary and biased.
You are a beautiful and awakened young woman, you are valuable and
bright.

Hope. Heart-banging hope. Help. Hell driven to it.

Weightless and alive again, if only for a moment.

Days that follow are shamed and long, you take up running to exhaust you.

More messages, same sender. Loud and authoritative, tender and persistent.

Nobody else knows where your brain has taken you but them. But you are here now, unmasked, accounted for, being pulled forward by a rope of desperate late night slobbering calls that without, you would have autopilot-slumped on the cold porcelain of a public bathroom.

There is not a night that passes where the words exchanged don't help you. Ease you. Humanise you. They cradle your battered brain to vow you will do the same for someone else at any cost. In your greatest weakness, they battled for your strength. You are here now, unmasked, accounted for, alive.

inner gold

Soften the shards
That broke you clean
Fresh and angry
As though they seem
Can be rounded as gems
Handed as souvenirs
To those who are yet to find light
In your old rotten fears.

resilience

Novelty is such the mind's addiction
Cravings for comfort
In things that breed emptiness
Feasting on feelings with the unfriendliest

                                    faces

But what if we traded to take from different places?
If we nourished our souls in ways we deserved
And picked softer tools to tickle our nerves
Cradled our minds in a sip of a sauce of its own brilliance
And found novelty in our mind's own source of resilience.

dysthymia

It is uncomfortable blunt language
No apology screens sincere enough
For the screams and swearing
Of what it's made me do
It circles on my tongue
Bitter furs and tangs of acid
As I repent on how this thing
That I lost the remote for
Could ever make you feel
I didn't love you
In the deepest way I could.

wrong spaces

Why does the guilt
Always hit so late?
Twist and rip
It breaks me in two
Still not half enough
Still too whole
To dive back into
Dizzying nausea
Fills me up more and
More
Spurting, bursting
All encompassed hurting
Still not half enough
Still too whole.

kindness

All that matters is kindness
I know it sounds obvious
But it's true
Think of all the bad things in the world
And then think of you
Think about all of the troubles you've faced
And then think of all the kind faces
That pulled you through
It's them that reminded
you of your power
And on the days you feel you've got little purpose
Remember as humans it's as basic as showering
Others with kindness
Compassion
Lashings
Of love
Regardless of race, sex, location, and material stuff
It's kindness in its simplest sense
That will take us from this dark present
Into a more hopeful, prospecting tense.

Your mind is biased
And your brain is blind
There's still a store of
            strength
Left in you to find

she must be fat

body part 1

It's April in London and you're smiling at your feet. Toes jumping up
and down gently, padding against the leather sole of wicker wedges.
It's your first day of your first job and the first time you've ever
ordered a coffee. 'Two skinny chai lattes please.'
A blonde woman, far too pretty to be fair, swings on her heels and
reaches for a wooden swizzling stick. She looks like she's got her shit
together, she's thin and tall and blonde and beautiful
and thin
and thin
and thin.

She's so thin.

You wish you could stand in that frame, all collarbones and angled
elbows, but you're on the wrong side of 5'9" with rounded thighs
and a well-cushioned overhang of tummy pressing out from your
jeans. You squish it back in, smooth out your ponytail and walk half
a block to work.

Everything is a clinical white, the walls, the backdrops, the shiny
Apple Mac mouses, the lights, everything down to the people and
their skin and the cyclical noise of clacking shoes.
You pick up the arm of a steamer and rush it over a crimson satin
dress, tickling the long sleeves down its seams and knock on the
dressing room door. Nervous.
'Yah, I'm ready.'

It's her and it's you, her and her long-limbed body – naked from the waist up, tiny pert boobs meeting your eyes like pins pricking balloons. She places her left hand on your forearm to balance, steps into the dress, and waits for you to zip it at the back.

When you get home you unzip yourself.

Knickers snake the legs of jeans that lay atop a faded Marks & Spencer's bra, the underwire poking to catch the cuffs of your old favourite jumper. You drop your jewellery – weightless coppered rings that have left green replacements, thin golden chains, a hair clip pushing back your sweaty fringe. Off. Just in case. Deep sigh, deeper breath out. You arch your back forwards, you've forgotten your socks. Ankles embrace and tango to fling them off in a finale. Hopeful. Palms, cradling your stomach, there is more to give. 'Have a quick wee.' Just in case, deep sigh, deeper breath out, hopeful.

Standing as a body, rosacea and bruises that paint Rorschach marks across the backs of your goose-pimpled thighs, just pure, finite flesh, your toes lift and tip with trepidation from bathroom tile to the familiar cold white skin of the scales. A number flashes and flits, undecided, jumping between aggressive differences, innocent to the wait of the worth and the worth of the weight. Static digits. Staring. There is more to give. There is more to understand. There is more to remembering the woman with the coffees and the girl and her naked body, there is more to you than what you think there should be less of. But still, as weeks turn over months and these moments feel like impressing years, you forget again in these alone minutes and all you know of yourself is a number.

stuff

I think the thing that really gets me
The thing that turns me green
      The thing that makes me really want to scream
Is if I took away the inches
The measurements, the weight
The half-cut-up potatoes
Left to grow cold on my plate
The thing that makes me angry
Makes me want to cry
Is I've always been much smaller
Than the way I've understood size

I've made up sticks of butter
That I've told myself I'm made of
And I've sold myself as bigger
Arched my arms wider than needed to cradle
This magnificent piece of magic
That keeps me all together
This stuff that I have pulled at
This stuff that I should've treasured
This stuff that in all these years
I've told myself is huge
Has simply been the shape
Of the holiest refuge
With every time I look back

Sometimes only just a year
I wonder why I waddled with
This disgusting faulting fear
There was not that much of me
There was just enough
There was cellulite and thighs
But there was also just this stuff

This stuff that wasn't ugly
This stuff that wasn't big
This stuff that was simply just me
Stretching to a woman from a kid
This stuff that I don't remember
Ever wishing there wasn't less of
But as I'm getting older
I can't stand it being the death of
My sense of reality
I only hope
I only pray
I'll start to see
If I look properly
There'll never be too much of me.

shoreditch house

She took one look at me and decided not to change her dress
Decided that even in her work clothes
They'd still serve further to impress
Him
The depression has started to kick in
I slipped in
To this
I slip into this
I slip in every time
She'll kiss him
Without changing her dress
And I'll kid her I'm still fine.

Oh Kale leaves
How you depress me
I only eat you
So boys want to
UNDRESS ME.

kale reprised
(two years later)

I've been eating a lot of chips
To fill out the dips in my hips
That your fingers used to press
Nothing but a starving urge
To spill out of the silhouette
You'd once undress.

wrigley's extra

The comparison's a killer
So much so it's gum for dinner
Why didn't god birth me thin

The god I love lives in this house
She's beautiful
But the god I hate force fed my mouth
With words about my figure
That's why tonight it's gum for dinner

I say god
But the voice isn't holy
It's the voices of memories
Of boys who shuddered to hold me
Strange men in the street who scolded me
Inner thoughts who offered me
Biscuits when I was sad not hungry
That's why tonight it's gum for dinner

Perhaps I've got the wrong idea
Praying to someone who isn't here
For more lithe limbs and straighter hair
Bowing solemnly to such unfair words
Because if he was real, he'd be a sinner
He couldn't last on gum for dinner

He'd have no power in his bones
His voice would shout in shadowed tones
And pass out before he could complain
The confliction of this strength for weakness
Has always driven me insane.

trump

Tell me, sir
Explain it loud and clear
Shout your most direct
Explicit fears
Scream them until
The decibels reach parallel
To the clang and clatter in my heart
Until you can rage each syllable
So pointedly you can throw your voice like a sharpened dart
And throw it for me
Speak for me
Times those fears by ten
Then times them by one hundred
And one thousand and again
Keep multiplying what shakes you
Until it becomes so monstrous
So tangible and noxious
That it no longer feels like fear
It just feels constant
Familiar
Monotonous
Like you've spent your life rehearsing
For a nightmare
As the understudy
Never quite enough for the part

Because you don't qualify as somebody
Like you've learnt every line
As though what you feel is fiction
And you'll never get the lead as someone
Whose script is written with conviction

Tell me, sir
Explain it loud and clear
Explain it so loudly my unborn daughter can hear
Project your voice into the future
If you can impregnate me with these lost morals
You're free to rape me just as quick
And then what happens if you conceive more than fear?
What happens if I don't want that kid?
Your future is bubble-wrapped
And I'm held punishable for it.
Try and tell me that you're scared
As you bang my head on the glass ceiling
And drag me by my hair
Through statements like
SHE ASKED FOR IT
I'm pretty sure I didn't …
Pretty sure I'm pretty more
Than a pretty face to be ignored

Tell me, sir
Explain it loud and clear

Because I'm lost
Wandered down too many paths
With no roads for me safe enough to cross
Without carrying my keys like a weapon
Been employed in too many places
Where I'm a disposable body on a ladder to step on

Tell me, sir
Mr, why are your Mrs'
Missing out?
Why do you consider us so little?
Who was the man that taught you
To grow into this man so bitter
Dishing out
What I can and cannot be?
Who was the man that showed you a lesser being
And why was that lesser being me?

filters

My eyes a little brighter
My teeth a little whiter
My skin a little clearer
And my hair
…accidentally a little greener
The contrast of the exposure
Is not one that's clearer
The definition of the portrait
Is one of a heavyweight
Photoshopper
VSCO-er
I feel pretty when I'm told I am
I feel petty when it's as cold as
I'm a barefaced liar
#NoFilter filter
A scared-faced beauty in disguise
A normal looking human being
But my profile picture has you surprised
As though it's an image I'd been dreaming
The resemblance is close
My jawline is still mine
And my nose is still my nose
But would I still be of anyone's desire
If I wasn't hidden behind Instagram's required
Mask?

The mask of a fool

The mask of the twenty-first-century cruel world

Or the mask of a self-conscious tryna be cool girl

Does it matter?

I still sit and pixelate

Digitally deliberate, curl into an aesthetic looking ball

Until my anxiety is a candidate for Britain's Next Top face of the
    intimidated

My idea of beauty was once so different

So why have I confined that wonder

Into an ugly 4x4 square of imprisonment?

That has parameters smaller than the size of my thighs and is
    duller than the natural gradient of my eyes

I sit back so often with a chest thudding sigh

Scrolling

Refreshing

Relentless tapping

All down to an art

And think

Since when did I ignore my own heart to hack at my own life?

And since when did I become an image to sell of a millennial
    with scraps of sanity as its price?

london pervs

I swear to god
I'll swear louder than the tops
Of my stretched swollen lungs
I'll scream 'til I'm blue
And tie knots in your slimy shallow tongues
I swear to god
It's quite a simple thing to grasp
That if you shout at me in the street
Or brush your hand against my arse
If you simmer me down to a piece of meat
I won't be the one falling to their knees
Put your whistles in your pockets
Force your eyes back in their sockets
Spin your heels and curve your tongues into a curl
I will only say this once so listen up:
You've picked the wrong girl.

women's tea

I went into a health food store
To buy some spring roll skins
And found myself instead
In an aisle of loose leaf tea tins

Digestion, anxiety, whatever your ailment
They were stacked in dozens of varieties
And foreign flagrant flavours

This one box caught my eye
Barbie brash bold pink
It read 'Women's Tea'
And I was lost on what to think
Stuff the patriarchy!
Stuff your colour-denoted sexes!
When were leaves vulnerable to this malarkey!
I bet it's even more expensive

So I marched with echoed stomps
And slammed it on the desk
Turns out some herbs are good for cramps
And some are good for men

So I pocketed my placards
And zipped my coat over my Pankhurst shirt
And thought before I spluttered statistics
I should have a cuppa first.

imposter

I have always thought
That people have commented on
My beauty
Because of my female appearance
As though my gender was a given
For physical applause
But never did I realise
That it could be because they found me beautiful
And yet when it's been suggested
That I'm not in proportion
I have felt unworthy
Of this gender at all
And panic unsure
In a male gaze
That tips me on a scale
Of which I always weigh too heavy
To know what's true.

hunger

Weighted by the weight of me
Weightless when I quickly eat
Forgetting all the bits I see
In the bathroom, only me
At the table I transport
To somewhere that I can't be caught
Ham-fisted with empty calories

Picking plates, pushed pieces
Straightened back, stretched out creases
Knife and fork, balanced crossed
Brain salivating into figures lost
What deliciousness it forces, fake
As the satiation is a masked empty
That is only weighted by the weight of me.

gift for a man

I'm scared that if things don't change
If I don't shout louder
I'll be met with a future daughter
Who will feel a pressure on her worth to shrink shorter
And I'll be responsible if I have to hear her say:

'How can I be so foolish
to sit with marble ham thighs
A masculine tone
Dilated pupils and tar-stained bone
And think someone might wish
Upon each passionate gesture I make
I might be his to kiss?'

Fingers that bend all but the middle
Dirtied language and eyes of white
Stand to a halt as each stranger approaches her at night
And as she struggles to find the compliment
It's their lurid advances that give her a twisted confidence

That no matter how tall she stands
She'll only be worthy of love
If she kneels, plain and thin
As a gift for a man.

How will I make her feel something new
When I've spent so much time feeling that that might be true?

sobriety

This present day
Has no tonic to dilute it
Uncarbonated calm
Eyes wide awake
That stare down old habits
Searching out new ones
Somewhat disappointed
To find present day.

cellulite (sells you heavy)

There is a fold beneath the crease
That haunts me with trepidation
And despite what preparation
Goes into each breakfast
It seems there is an infiltration
This breeding nation
Of fat
That crawls and creeps between my legs
Regardless of what weight I shed
The bicycle motions I do in bed
Are relentless
Where is the redemption
For those who exercise?
My thighs
Jesus Christ the size
It should not be fair
Cellulite, sells you heavy
Cells from genes I was not ready to grow
Jeans that are unable to grow with me
They exhaust me from the source of me
They heckle me from each freckle on me
And if I could take a biological eraser
Remove these frustrating chubby placers
I thought I would
I tried to tell myself each dimple is a smile along my skin

A lightning bolt breaking from within
The happiness of a chicken nugget
Is a small white rocket
That bends to be a part of me
Pretends to be a piece of me
But nothing that small can be the defeat of me
And that's why I stopped wishing them away
I can't tell you how free it feels to prod them
And be okay
To look at them and be fine
To open up and say
My body stretched to make this space
And these tiny imperfections are mine.

fat

Please
I beg you
Don't touch that
That handle that you want to grab
That protruding piece of mass
Please don't touch that
Don't remind me of my dinner
Then absolve your arms as though I am thinner
Please don't touch that

Please don't touch that and then pretend it isn't there
Yet still give me an unapproving stare
When I reach for seconds
Please, I'm asking nicely
Don't touch that even politely
Don't laugh at all my icons
And say I could be her if my thighs were gone
If my legs were tight and long
Please don't touch that

Don't command my skin like you are proud
When publically you are loud
About how there's too much
But somehow in bedroom whispers
Your language dissolves straight into touch
Please don't touch that

If you can't see it's me

I have spent too many years
Stroking my own thigh to knee
To know what's there
And if for a sober second
Deep within your heart's compassion
You think you might have capacity
To hesitate my weight and then scream sexual passion

Please for the love of god don't touch that

Don't touch me at all

Because I spend too much time weighing myself

To wait to see that you're such a fool

To touch me

And not see the pain that's looking back

Don't touch me when you know how I feel and you call that
   feeling fat

Please don't touch that.

body part 2

He touches you. *He* is no one in particular in your recollection, he has become many faces. Faces that interchange within your memory upon recalling any which one of these stories you begin to tell your friends and then retreat. You say nothing. Your face grows depressed at the concept and with your same face you feel disgusting. As hands paw along your flesh you are so aware of all that you are. How that might be unattractive. How if it feels uncomfortable to you, how grotesque it must feel from the palms of another. Past experience has told you this anxiety is worthy. Past faces have furrowed eyebrows and then widened and pursed lips to disgruntle at the space within which you take up. You push it from your brain. Relax. Remember to relax. Remember that the reason why you have a disjointed relationship with your body is because you can't relax. But you can't. Popping candy synapses wet between your ears and fire off all manner of heart spasms and unease and short breaths and weighted defeat.

He asks you to say things, to do things.
You say them, you do them.

In the same instance that you choose not to remember his name, because he has had so many, you choose not to remember the list of bursting speech bubbles that blew from between your lips with syruped saliva, and even though they are old, they sound new, and even in your memory, you say them again.

Dutifully.

This, surely, is how you relax.

Listening, observing, serving. Taking action and control from some-
one more confident, more experienced. You let him touch you, your
body shivers with an immoderate buzz of panic that he confuses for
excitement, quietly disguising against your own will, relearning your
own body. These are not mixed messages, this is the only language
that you know. Quietly in inner turmoil. Nothing here is obvious or
certain. It's just uncomfortable. But that's how it always is and how
it's always been and you are sure will always be and the reason why
you feel so disconnected and afraid and ashamed of this experience
is because all that he's touching, all that he's grabbing already dis-
tastefully is

Fat.

You feel every inch of yourself squirm. Suddenly everything is
obvious and everything is certain.

Everything is wrong.

You are stuck in the flash of your own realisation, hands reaching for
duvet, fingers being bent back upon themselves with his.

His pace quickens and you assume a noise to the action, you heard
it once in a film your friend's older brother showed you, a stale but
stuck reference point, so you echo it. Echo, echo, echo.

You find yourself here time and time again, telling yourself that
you're putting yourself through exposure therapy, telling yourself
you deserve it, telling yourself this is good, telling yourself *this is
normal*, this is normal, you have put yourself here, you have been
complicit this far, ignore why, ignore your discomfort, ignore the

fact you realised this on the journey here and you've since tried to leave and you've asked to leave, you've asked politely and then you've said bluntly and then you've booked a cab and then it's been cancelled, but your brain is so heavy with hate and self-doubt and confusion that you've forgotten you've said those things. You've forgotten he's noticed, you've forgotten he's said no to your no, you've forgotten he's played into your weakness. You've forgotten who you are. So you listen to his rhetoric and tell yourself that your body will be yours to own once someone has put a price on it that you're willing to buy it back for. But you never seem to. You never want to buy it back because it is offered in such unrecognisable packaging, that you hope the last transaction means it's yours no longer.

'Please, please, just take me. Take it all from me and let me no longer be responsible.'

Your responsibility feels excruciating and complicated and exhausted. You had tried so many times to free your body but now it's all so enmeshed you're lost for how.
You're lost. You're tired. You're vulnerable. Unknowingly, because of those things, your brain is whimpering on behalf of your body:

'Please, please, just take me. Take it all from me and let me no longer be responsible.'

Until one day a man does, in a way that you feel is absolute, that feels so concrete, he takes it in such a way that it is no longer yours to bargain with. He stamps on it. You have been here before but until this moment you don't realise the danger. He touches your fat body and tells you what it is, he drags it, tells you he's caressing, and no matter how many times you question it in your head, question it aloud, say you are tired, say you are asleep, actually fall asleep, dream vivid nightmares prematurely, wake up and feel his breath inhale your protests, he hands back half the worth that's half the worth of what you were afraid of that you owned. Nobody knows, you never mention it. Just him. Just you. In retrospect, just all of you. Just a night where you entered a room feeling fat and left feeling much heavier. You wonder for months, 'Would this have happened if I was skinny and confident and could just say no?' And one day you hope, it's still not yet, you can turn around and see that you'd always said no, and one day you'll see that no rolls or cellulite can count as witnesses, not because it wasn't true, but because they weren't there.

bodies

You can turn them off and on
You can make them fat then thin
You could do a lot of courageous stuff
If we gave them enough space to breathe in
The prodding is an obvious hurdle
And the feeling your stomach feels
When it's near ready for its contents to curdle
The thighs leaning back
Trying to impression a gap
Waiting for a waistline
To waste away
It's all a trap
Squeezing anxiously at your face
And your nail beds being the last thing that you could taste
Wondering if down there is tight enough
Wondering if your jaw line is slight enough
Enough
These bodies that we've made
Are much stronger than we ever knew
Before we saw what we'd face
They're bigger than our thoughts
And sturdier than our psyche
It's a miracle that they can't speak
Because if they could they'd shout
WHY CAN'T YOU JUST LIKE ME

I'm doing so much stuff
That you don't ever see
I'm forcing organs and beating breaths
I'm keeping us alive, quietly

                And all you do is complain

What's sad is it's fair and often contrite

We do all of this personal grieving

Even though we know that it's not right

But how we can we change our learnt perceptions

When the thoughts that we breed are invited to receptions

Daily

To listen to our own lack of worth

When our bodies are trailed through media's dirt

When school is not about grades but the length of your skirt

If I'm half a size smaller will I be liked first

I've only had liquids so how do I quantify thirst

When sex isn't about love but 'how much did it hurt?'

When do we remember our worth

It really is worth it

To think about how we're working

Not to fixate on the vanity parade

That we're constantly scrolling and old school surfing

This stuff we consume is so fleeting

When there's stuff that supports us a whole life time

That keeps us breathing

And we shun it

Tell us in a lottery of bodies

Everyone else has won it

But us

That's crazy

Crazy that we fill ourselves with so little that we're hazy

We can't think properly

Because our diets are so light

That our concentration's sloppy

That our skin is so grim

Because we drink ourselves so wobbly

Our head bangs so bad that we can't help but think somberly

We're chain smoking at the sight of a sky

So you can just pause for a moment

And on your own sigh 'what's wrong with me?'

That is not a good use of a body

It should be angry and charging

Not knackered and starving

It has so much power to be starting

Anything we drive it towards

Past a distraction of how we treated it before

Past us ignoring its own personal encore

To be reignited

For the love of whatever is good

What the hell are we fighting?

When the skin we're in

Holds us closer than our next of kin

Ever could

Why are we fighting against something

That gods never would?
Why are we bowing to a new fate
That our muchness is weighed up to
To the weight that we weigh
That our sumptuous ethereal smart humanness means
We'll always think we are paupers
But have the same bodies as queens

I am not yours
To be beautiful for
I do not clothe myself
To be adored
The most finite of Knowledge
That I can Keep steady
Is that I am mine
To feel sexy.

she must be an adult

age

You are eight years old, tiny toes and fingers have clambered up onto the sofa and sprawled, soft head first, onto the lap of your grandfather. You unpick a packet of Chewits cautiously, popping a pink one in your mouth and clammy handedly produce a yellow one for him. In between each chomp he smiles

'One day you'll be as old as me, I never knew I'd be as old as me.'

It frightens you. Your eyes close and you sigh. He pauses, rushes his hands through your hair and grins

'Think of all the adventures you're going to have. I wonder who you'll marry? I wonder if that man has been born yet, where is he in the world? I wonder who you'll decide to be. Isn't that exciting! You just don't know yet but I know it's all going to be brilliant.'

It sticks with you much longer than he ever let it be a thought. It sticks with you until those questions grow around your ribs and seep into your lungs, you push them out past sighs and lengthen them to breaths. You let them grow to become place holders for answers.

Your mother and your grandmother sit across from you on that same sofa, you are now fourteen. The dips and peaks of their profiles are identical to yours, their fidgets mirror, their breaths beat similar. You think of all the adventures *they've* had, the mistakes they've made and the promises they've kept. The women they've become. The powerhouses and strong-willed statues, the no-nonsense and all loving, the triers and succeeders, the women.

You open up the place holders your grandfather first created and stamp them there as quotation marks, these are the women you too will become. Growing up, in that pause, is suddenly less daunting.

But before you know it it's 3 a.m. on a Monday and you're typing cover letters with one hand and spoon feeding yourself baked beans on penne pasta from your bed, there is an old soup stain on your top making friends with a much older red wine stain, there is chipped nail varnish on your veneers from gnashing, forty-three unread text messages, fifteen new Tinder matches and one series of Master of None replaying over and over on an infinite loop in the background. The room smells tired. You fall asleep, everything left in its place.

Four hours later, in your mother's blazer and your grandmother's dress, shoes that your father once bought you and a necklace you 'borrowed' from somebody else's jewellery box, a little girl looks up at you with her pearl drop eyes of hope and wonder, unstuck momentarily from the moving landscape out the commuter train window and she surveys you. You smile at her as your ovaries trick you with a pang. She nestles her face behind her hands and takes another peek through her digits. She is wary. She looks at you, really looks, gaze fixated, and sees you, wholesomely, as an adult. When did this happen? It all happened so fast. And did it really happen at all? You want to shake her, lift off your blazer and show her your pyjama top still worn underneath, pull out the small bunny rabbit toy that you hide in your handbag for comfort, read her the panicked text messages to your mother that scream

I don't know how to be an adult.

Scroll through countless photos of you in Ladbroke Grove just last week with red eyes and greasy hair, ham-fisted with receipts from a drunken hotel night stay, empty packets of cigarettes splayed across the table, searching for loose change to get the train to work, to get *this* train to work. 'Shit, I'm going to work.'

Shit, I'm an adult and nobody told me.

goldman sachs

Sometimes it doesn't go right
The wayward nights
You imagined
The taxi trips with strangers
Paying bar bills with party favours
Sometimes it isn't a film
No vignette close enough
To cradle you within
Its dark expanse and tell you that
Not all of these men want adventure
Not all of them are character studies
Not all of them think you're funny and smart
Not all of them want to hear about your father
Not all of them want to be a consensual partner
Sometimes it doesn't go right
And sometimes it's best
To go home and straight to bed
Instead of exploring the night.

I'll be home in the morning

This is a mistake
But something in my loins says yes
Something allows him to undress
Something takes me straight to bed
And that something doesn't live in my head
It sits a pain within my chest
Beyond a place where secrets rest
It's dark and I don't like it there
It's packed with secrets and overstuffed
Yet what it screams that mutes me deaf
The most blatant entry I misread
Says simply:

> Don't do this
> When all you want to be is loved.

too young

It drizzled down
Precious and thin
Weaving matted through my hair
My neck crooked over the side of the bath
And your shoes gone from the bottom of the stairs.
I must've been
Only fifteen
But that nausea was centuries old
My nose plugged with the scent of your cheap aftershave
And the shower head spitting out cold
You said I no longer tasted much like love
And my hips were the wrong side of wide
I tried to wash you like dirt from off my red mottled skin
And let you sink with the suds down the pipes
But you left a scum that stuck to the sides.

say you're sorry

She was nearly my age
When she first heard your name
It will take until her age
For me to walk away
And now at your age
Everything's too late.

they came out and I stayed in

All my friends are gay
And I wouldn't have it any other way
Except on Friday nights
When I've got no one to get off with.

E1W 3SS/Billy

Come up
And come down with me
Taste your figures
On the furs of your teeth
Youth might be wasted on the young
But slip into this neon vulnerability
And we'll be wiser when the morning comes
That ravages on our undressed mess
But sip on the warm-ending edges of the sleepless sun
And we'll be wiser before we're wasted again
On all the thoughts we slurred and acted on
Come up
And come down with me

We can't do this when we're thirty.

pint-sized

I've got this thing with kids on trains
I sit there mesmerised
Watching the silhouettes of flashing landscapes
Reflect like magic in their eyes
Watching their tiny bodies perform
Pint-sized
Attempts at behaving
Swaying
With each stop

I'd quite like to swap

Because I can't remember anymore
Of how it felt to take up such little space
And for that to be a good thing
For my learning and naivety
Grabbing hands and misused words
To be a sweet thing
How it felt to be a glaring honest thing
I wish back then I would have taken note

Could've scraped together all the statements I didn't know to
. sugar coat
And kept them in my armour
Kept their tangy sour taste and smile at them with the same charm

A new little girl now has
With my old grabbing hands
I want to shake her to realize
That her mischief is perfect
And that growing up is a downsize
Just stay put,
And only move as the train moves.

whatsapp

In these times
Of double ticks
Last seen minutes
And ghosting pricks
Just text your girls
And save your breath.

roots of them/sorry, jacob

They're so beautiful
And even when I feel not so
They still remain
And there's a beauty in knowing
That when it can't be self-proclaimed
It can still be breathed in, seen and attained
That those around you's beauty always escapes your change
Well sort of, same same
But different
You see it as a caged reminder of wrongdoings
An unmeasurable imprisonment
It thrashes a hotter whip
Lashes of a slobbering trip
As you lick your lips
And taste the saltiness of their beauty
Instead of smelling it as sweet
Sometimes the feelings we mistake
As a clarity on others darkness
Screaming solemn swears that
The harmless are heartless
Is us projecting our fear of losing beauty
Of power, of wonderment, of worth
But for what it's worth
What I've learnt
Is to swallow it down and accept it

Pick up a tougher smile as you exit
Pick up what you admire and inspect it
Until you understand why you respect it
Take time to realise the roots of them are the roots of you
And you'll think yourself beautiful too.

kids

Our bones stuck like honey
Silken gestures grazing ground
As we flew over handlebars
And relished in dotting our bloodied scars with the same tiny
     digits that made shapes with carbon-backed stars.
The nonsense made sense in its cherry-rich taste of speaking a
     language of pulling funny faces.
The fear of inferior was nothing but a shifting canvas that smelt
     like summer
Shedding our winter skin to become a
Firecracker of innocence
An uncorrupted, feverishly disruptive
Blazing ball of wonder
And when we expanded from its amber shell
Spitting sparks as we embraced the swell
Each filament of learning spun a grand farewell
And spoke a greeting to the less bright
Other side of where those taller weren't glowing
I'm sure we'd never have grown up if
We'd been told where we were going.

forever

Can you be related to a soulmate?
Can you be born into fate?
Can two nodding identical profiles
Bear such growing worldly weight?
I sympathise my all
With those who need to find the one
When all of my searching
Stopped when I begun
Because the child in me has always known
The only one I need
Will always be my mum.

baby ella

Fingernails flat like scraps of seashells
Pull and paw at a tide of softness
Scratching out unthought feelings
Human hieroglyphics
Of maternity
As these tiny digits cling to me
Until I breathe out a shape of my heart
And imagine it as your own
No longer frightened
Knowing that all that's within me
Hands like yours one day
Will hold and call home.

adult

You are shoulder to someone's waist in rows of black. A ceiling above you fifteen times as many feet as you stand and as ornate and detailed as the Skechers trainers you'd begged to wear today but had been denied. Mum said they were inappropriate. You didn't know what that meant. They were black and silver, just the same in your mind's eye as every outfit you'd ever seen in Disney shows that were worn to funerals. You take a pew, bashfully battle your lungs for song and try to ignore the sobs. Grief is an unexplored, unexplained alien that greets you at a coffin, offers out its hand in introduction and pulls away quick enough for you to remain unacquainted properly. You go to offer it small talk but it is already someone else's turn. You sit at a wake and watch people get drunk, laugh and tell stories, cry quietly safe in the knowledge that you, a small child who knows nothing, is only watching. There is something inside of you that begs to feel sad, to understand. You pull and push for tears, fists banging against your eyes to see stars, wishing for water but nothing comes. You feel your age for the very first time in a way that you'll always remember. You are eight. You feel young. You feel untainted. You feel like today is a controlled blip in the universe being driven by a car that will keep on going to a place where you'll never have to return. You only need to stand at this place once. You tell yourself, despite your known and sure naivety, with such total confidence that today is not normal and will not ever have to happen again. The world that you know is not made to allow for such capacity for sadness. The world that you know is so new it cannot end.

Ten years later, then eleven and twelve, you put on a dress that is black and a necklace that is silver, you have tried on eight different things still not knowing what is appropriate. You always end up in the same dress. You settle, smooth it down, you cry. You have been to many of these now, you even know the words to hymns you proudly once shrugged off. Everything hurts and yet everything is weightless.

Almost too close to feeling the blood run and rush away from your body, almost lifeless, but flowing into a room that is pulsing and cursing that it's still alive and desperately attempting to meditate around the idea that being here, portrait not horizontal, is a lucky thing. None of you feel lucky. All of you wish just for a moment you were horizontal. You feel grief.

It smacks you soberly until you reach for a glass and engage in a chat that brings you to reminiscing. Only recounting the good things. Feeling your soul filled with countless anecdotes about a person you wished you had called and retold with them but now you can't. Everyone pretends that what others share is special but only what they share is special to them because they can't share it with the only person that would laugh loudest, who knows every face in the room, because they aren't also holding a glass. They're not pressed up on the bar side, or holding your hand after school, or silently judging your hangover. They're gone, replaced with a silhouette of grief.

Days after, every time, you feel much older. Much wiser. So much taller than the child that once only wished for sparkly trainers and a car that kept on revving. You feel, for the first time, again and again, like an adult. Growing up becomes not of broken romances, not of grades, not of jobs, not of pounds of flesh or those in the bank and not of expectations. It even, for a moment, that flits subconsciously, is not of trying to stay alive, not of thinking back on all the times you had pondered or tried to not be. It's of being purposeful. Of making so goddamn sure that when your time comes there are stories and laughter, that there are people who know they were loved, that there were successes to recount, that there was advice that was shared, that there were parties and chats and changes. That whatever room at whatever time you leave deaf, you are certain that you know if you could hear anything at all, that what is walked out beside you and what is spluttered and sobbed and sung generously, is that you had love and that you had purpose.

Months after, those sentiments seem trivial again, almost forgotten in the ether of everyday life, of recovery and acceptance. It's your birthday. You are standing on a chair, holding the hems of a dress your younger self would have dreamt of and you say, simply and so drunkenly it's almost incoherent, 'Thank you all for being here, thank you for giving me the life I have, I love you.' You step down to walk away as people whoop and cheer and laugh and grin and chink their glasses until you can float to the back of the bar and cry.

The funny thing in all of this, the thing so funny it's often quite difficult to find laughable, is the banality of everything you feel in what initially comes at you with such a distinguished pang as though it'll never come again, but it does. It does and it does and it does. It keeps on smacking your brain with a heavy punch that suggests you weren't expecting it until you start to study it. Until there it is again, that feeling, that anxiety, that kiss, that argument, and so you involuntarily laugh once your head bruise has simmered down to nearly skin colour and you roll your eyes and let out this lip shaking smile of a giggle that's really a sigh. That moment of realisation, suddenly in your twenties, that the last ten years have been on a cyclical calendar of emotion. Heartbreak, terror, grief, unworthiness, fatness, stupidity, relief, euphoria. You still have absolutely no idea what to do with them, what accent they speak with until you've heard them again, what weight they hold until they're thrust upon you, what bellowing bone-cringing laugh of a noise that will seep from within the depths of your lungs once the end of the loop comes round again and you realise.

You realise the most marvellous thing, the most life-affirming, presence-keeping bit of it all, is you're absolutely definitely without a doubt not supposed to know how to feel or how to think upon those feelings, nobody else does around you either. Not even those who suggest they do and not even you on a Tuesday night with a glass of wine feeling philosophical and wise do. You're in this circuit now and the best you can do is give it a nod every time you re-recognise an old thought introducing itself as unstale. You've done it, really. The foundations are built. Now all that is left is to choose how you respond knowing how things turned out the last time you didn't know you had choice.

seaweed – for grandad

Before it was the future
Before it was my brain
Before it was gun reforms
Before it was climate change
Before it was heartbreak
Before it was potential
Before it was plastics in the sea
Before it was existential
Before it was family illness
Before it was personal tax
Before it was the price of houses
Before it was the price of a wax
Before I knew what really worried me

It was seaweed

Long gangly tendrils of green
Wefts of Medusa's very own wig, had you asked me
Evil slithery things
That clasped around my ankle
Left in the water by one of Poseidon's own vandals
My two innocent limbs braving a leisurely dangle
Until I decided the holiday was cut short
Because I was convinced I was up next to be strangled

Before it was my weight
Before it was purpose
Before it was societal standards
Before it was junior nurses
Before it was Donald Trump
Before it was dairy alternatives
Before it was the state of my skin
Before it was what state we're in with the Conservatives
Before it was 'What do you mean no WIFI?'
Before it was Twitter trolls
Before it was feeling like a fraud
Before it was over-ambitious goals

It was seaweed

Before it was the effects of contraception
Before it was terrorism
Before it was the end of *Inception*
Before it was faux feminism

It was seaweed

My first experience of the unknown
I ran sandy toed
Into the only arms I trusted
'Grandad!' I cried, flustered
'I can't go back in there!'

Frightened, I was pointing at the sea
Whilst he was laughing at me
Not in a way that I know now
No, he was giggling kindly
'Darling, it's just grass,
Come on, I'll show you.'
And he did that gorgeous thing
When as a kid adults pretend to throw you
And then catch you
And bring you back to their chest
And you sniff in a nuzzle
As they kiss your head

And everything melts away

All my worries were just bits of grass in the sea
All the hope that I needed was him smiling at me
All the knowledge I had
Had come from his brain
And despite all of my anxieties
That thought keeps me sane

Someone will always know more
Someone will always be grinning
Someone will always be willing
Someone will hold you
When it all seems too big

Someone will show you
The real size that it is
Yes, the world's scary
My god is it tough
But there will always be someone
Who loves you enough
To try and take it away
And that someone
Made you someone enough
To be your own someone
To make sure you're okay

Before it was seaweed
It was blissful and calm
But I'd cradle an ocean of watery weeds
To know that I'd always be safe in your arms.

expectations

Am I soft enough
Am I tame enough for you?
Does my name taste sweet enough
Are my convictions lame enough for you?
Am I seen enough
And herded by you?
What is it to be a good woman
In a world of bitter truths?
Am I soft enough?
Am I half enough for you?

yellow cabs

I had always claimed
Regret could never know me
Regret could never drive me
I would not allow myself to wallow in his punishing fear

As I sit and count out my last quarters
He offers his hand to take them
Pocketing a shrapnel token
And taxis me to JFK.

hospital visits

No colour is quite its best self
Insipid yellows and half greys
Walls flake
With an old damp regret
Not yet brave enough to peel off entirely
The din of wheels and microwave meals
Clack and click unconfidently
And as your throat constricts
And you feel sick to your stomach
You can't help but wonder
If it's the grip of somebody else's death
Trying to talk to you.

You will choose to not give yourself the best chance. It will often not feel like a choice but an act of punishment. A self-declaration that you are not worthy of the good or the exciting, to feel proud or to feel smart or to feel good enough. You push away friendships that fulfil you and enter relationships that break you, you continue toxic cycles of bad habits and behave with such an aggressive recklessness that to those on the outside you seem a fool. A fool that doesn't care. But you do, you care so deeply that when you are full you feel you have no choice but to spit everything out. To excel in purging all that you are and all that you hate and all that you have and all that you love. It seems nonsensical in the brief and dark and tired moments of reflection. A reflection in which you cannot recognise the planes of your own face and the curves of your own mind.

In the end, it all boils down to these minutiae, these tiny fleeting moments, these vignettes. They all pass you by so quickly. Some of them feel as though they will, they feel as weightless as the seconds they are often administered in. But all considered and put together, these are what shape you. Pain you, excite you, almost break you. All just moments you thought could never be beaten in their insanity. Memories and makings of this jaggedy soul that may well be mad but is the greatest body of strength you'll ever know.

acknowledgements

The thanks I have to give could do with borrowing the pages of a whole new book. Without the incredible, resilient, emotionally intelligent, insane, beautiful people I've met in the last few years, I'd never have had the courage to endure these stories and emotions let alone write about and share them. I am forever grateful and in awe, the biggest thank yous to -

To my family. For supporting me on a ridiculous journey that has always swerved getting 'a real job' and believing in me and my wildest dreams. Nothing ever feels too big because of you and in turn every win is done for you.

To my boys, all of you. Adrian, Jack, Finn, Will, Toby P and Luke. Without your smarts and love, without your wit and kindness, without the wine and wayward nights and late night panicked phone calls, without your unconditional support I'd not be here and I'd not be me. Thank God I did something right in a past life to get you as my brothers. Thank you for offering out spaces within you when all I've wanted to do is give up.

To my women. To Shannon, to Scarlett, to Beth, to Steph, to Tirion, to Sophie, to DJ and KB. For loving me despite my terrible taste in men. For pushing me when I've screamed defeat. For constantly showing me the power and brilliance of womanness. I love you so damn much.

To Abigail for believing in me, for putting up with me and being the agent I once hoped and dreamed and prayed as a little girl that I'd one day have. You are the absolute best.

To Rachel, to Celia and all the wonderful people at HQ. Thank you
SO much for trusting in *She Must Be Mad* and trusting in me. I'm so
glad we got to make this together.

And to mum. 'MORE'. More than you'll ever know.